Think Fast. Think Smart. Think Bold. Think Beyond.

Marako Marcus

Published by Marako Marcus, 2025.

Copyright Page

While every precaution has been taken in the preparation of this book, the publisher assumes no responsibility for errors or omissions, or for damages resulting from the use of the information contained herein. No part of this book may be reproduced, stored in a retrieval system, or transmitted in any form or by any means, electronic, mechanical, photocopying, recording, or otherwise, without the prior written permission of the publisher, except as permitted by applicable copyright law. The information and views expressed in this book are those of the author and do not necessarily reflect the views of any organization or entity. All names, characters, and incidents in this book are fictitious. Any resemblance to real persons, living or dead, is purely coincidental.

Think Fast. Think Smart. Think Bold. Think Beyond.

From Quick Wins to Bold Breakthroughs—Master Modern Thinking

First Edition, January 1, 2025.

Copyright © 2025 Marako Marcus.

Written by Marako Marcus.

Introduction: Thinking at the Speed of Leadership

Over my 25 years as a management consultant, assessment center assessor, and executive coach, I've worked with leaders at every level—from bright-eyed up-and-comers to seasoned executives staring down crises. There's one question I've been asked more than any other: "Do we have the right talent?"

It's a question that shapes billion-dollar decisions. Leaders lose sleep over it, boards demand answers, and HR departments scramble to justify their recommendations. But here's the irony: When we assess talent in action, we often uncover a glaring problem that no one wants to admit. It's not about how smart people are, how many degrees they've racked up, or how many hours they log at their desks. The real issue? They don't think fast enough. They don't think smart enough. And they don't think strategically enough to meet the demands of today's business landscape.

Let me give you an example.

THE BOARDROOM MIRAGE

A few years ago, I ran an assessment center for a group of leaders at a multinational corporation. These were the so-called "cream of the crop"—handpicked successors to the C-suite. They were sharp, polished, and had impressive resumes. But once we placed them in high-pressure simulations—crisis scenarios, rapid decision-making exercises, and complex stakeholder negotiations—the cracks began to show.

One leader, tasked with making a decision under time constraints, froze. He spent 15 minutes second-guessing himself, terrified of being wrong. Another took a bold stance but failed to consider the broader strategic implications, alienating half the room. Yet another was so focused on impressing their peers that they missed critical details altogether.

These weren't incompetent people. They were highly capable professionals who had simply never been taught how to think under fire. They weren't prepared to pivot, adapt, or balance the tactical and strategic demands of modern leadership.

THE LEADERSHIP GAP

Here's the uncomfortable truth: Leadership is no longer about knowing the answers. It's about asking the right questions, adapting on the fly, and making smart, bold decisions—fast. The world moves too quickly for hesitation, over-analysis, or rigid thinking. Today's leaders need to think like sprinters, strategists, and innovators—all at once.

But too often, we train our leaders to play by outdated rules. We reward them for following established processes and maintaining the status quo. We forget that the real game is about speed, adaptability, and boldness.

This book was born out of those observations. It's for anyone who wants to close the gap between where they are and where they need to be. It's for leaders who want to think faster, act smarter, and lead with courage.

WHY THINKING MATTERS More Than Ever

Let's be clear: Thinking isn't some fluffy, intellectual exercise. It's your competitive edge. In today's world, where AI, market disruptions, and shifting global dynamics are rewriting the rules, the ability to think strategically, tactically, and creatively is what separates leaders from followers.

You can have the best team, the most innovative product, and a stellar strategy. But if you can't think on your feet when things go sideways—or think deeply when the stakes are high—you're doomed to mediocrity.

This book is your antidote.

WHAT YOU'LL LEARN

In the chapters ahead, you'll discover practical strategies to enhance your thinking in every dimension of leadership:

- Think Fast: Learn how to make decisions under pressure without breaking a sweat.
- Think Smart: Sharpen your analytical skills to find clarity in complexity.
- Think Bold: Develop the courage to challenge assumptions and take calculated risks.
- Think Beyond: Expand your perspective to see opportunities others miss.

Each chapter is packed with real-world examples, actionable tools, and no-nonsense advice. This isn't about theories or buzzwords. It's about practical strategies you can implement today to elevate your leadership game.

THE BOTTOM LINE

I've seen what happens when leaders don't rise to the occasion. Teams flounder, opportunities vanish, and organizations stagnate. But I've also seen what's possible when leaders step up—when they think with clarity, speed, and boldness. They inspire trust, create momentum, and drive extraordinary results.

So, if you're ready to think differently—if you're tired of outdated playbooks and want to sharpen your edge—this book is for you. It's time to rethink how we think. Let's get to work.

Strategy 1: The 3L Method

The business world doesn't have time for slow learners or people who take forever to catch on. If you want to succeed in today's fast-paced, high-stakes environment, you need to think quickly, deeply, and strategically—and it starts with the 3L Method: Learn, Link, Leverage.

Let's break it down.

LEARN – ABSORB INFORMATION Like a Sponge

There's no excuse for not being on top of what's happening in your industry. The first step in any leadership decision is learning. I don't care how much you already know. If you're not actively learning—you're falling behind.

When I was coaching a senior executive last year, he'd been in the same company for 15 years. Smart guy, no doubt about it. But he had this habit of operating in a bubble, relying on outdated knowledge. He didn't bother learning new trends, new technologies, or new strategies. The result? His ideas were stale. He missed the signs that disruption was on the horizon. He struggled to keep up with younger, faster-moving competitors.

Here's the problem: In the age of information, learning is no longer optional. If you want to be a leader, you need to absorb new data, new insights, new trends. And you need to do it fast. Skimming is your best friend—you don't have time for deep dives on every topic. Start with the headlines, then dive deeper into the essentials. Know what's critical for your business and your industry. Your ability to absorb knowledge quickly is directly tied to your ability to act quickly.

But here's the catch—learning isn't just about memorizing facts. It's about knowing how to process information rapidly, evaluate it critically, and move forward with it. You're not in school anymore. Don't just memorize for the test. Learn to adapt and keep your knowledge relevant.

LINK – BUILD CONNECTIONS Between What You Know

Once you've learned something new, the next step is to link it to what you already know. This is where many leaders falter. They think of knowledge as this siloed, isolated thing. "I know about marketing," they say, "so I'll only apply that knowledge to marketing." Wrong. Knowledge isn't valuable until you link it to other areas of expertise. If you're not linking your learning to existing knowledge, you're just accumulating data, not creating real value.

Let's take a scenario I saw during an assessment center. A candidate was brilliant in marketing but had zero idea how his department's decisions impacted the finance team. In a simulation, he came up with an excellent marketing campaign—but he failed to link that to the bottom line. He didn't consider cost, revenue impact, or ROI. Why? Because he wasn't thinking beyond his narrow expertise.

Leaders need to connect dots. When you learn something new, always ask yourself: How does this fit into the broader picture? How does this tie into the objectives of other departments? How can I apply this information in a way that influences multiple areas of the business?

Take another example: During a recent coaching session with a mid-level manager, she'd learned all about AI tools but wasn't sure how to implement them. When we discussed it further, she realized that AI could be integrated into her customer service team to enhance efficiency. She had the knowledge, but it was the linking of that knowledge to customer experience that made all the difference. She didn't just learn AI; she learned how to apply it.

Here's the bottom line: Knowledge without context is useless. Learn it. Link it. Apply it. It's that simple.

LEVERAGE – USE WHAT You've Learned to Drive Action

Learning and linking are useless unless you can leverage what you know to create real-world outcomes. This is where too many leaders fall short. They spend all their time consuming information and reflecting on it, but they fail to act on it. Don't be that leader.

During a leadership development program I facilitated, I watched an executive team go through a business simulation where they were asked to respond to a market crisis. They had all the information they needed—but they couldn't pull the trigger. They hesitated. They overthought. They were so bogged down in analysis that they missed the opportunity. The crisis worsened. They failed to capitalize on the moment.

Here's the hard truth: Knowledge is only valuable when you apply it. And to do that, you have to be able to act. It's about making decisions in the face of uncertainty. It's about pulling the trigger even when the full picture isn't clear.

In my own experience, the most successful leaders I've worked with don't waste time overthinking. They've mastered the art of leveraging knowledge quickly to make decisions, solve problems, and seize opportunities. They've learned how to turn insights into action, and they do it fast.

In one of my favorite coaching examples, a CEO was facing a market challenge with a competitor. She quickly learned about their strategy, linked it to her own company's strengths, and within days, launched a campaign that disrupted the competition. She leveraged her knowledge and made a bold, impactful move. And guess what? It worked.

The 3L Method—Learn, Link, Leverage—works because it forces you to act on what you know. It prevents paralysis by analysis and moves you from thought to execution. The more you practice this method, the faster and smarter you'll become at making decisions and taking action.

WHY IT WORKS: ACTIONABLE, Effective, and Fast

The 3L Method works because it's grounded in the real-world needs of modern leadership: speed, clarity, and impact. In today's business world, you can't afford to take weeks to learn something new or wait months to apply it. If you want to stay ahead of the competition, you need to think fast, act decisively, and learn continuously.

Here's the beauty of it: The 3L Method doesn't just help you make smarter decisions faster; it also empowers your teams to do the same. When you lead by example, you set the pace for everyone else. The faster you think, the faster your team will think. The quicker you act, the quicker they'll act. The more you learn, the more they'll learn.

Let's make it real: You've got a meeting coming up where the stakes are high. You need to present a strategic plan to your board, but there's little time for preparation. Do you freeze? Do you stumble through? Or do you think fast, link your insights, and leverage your knowledge to create a bold move? The 3L Method gives you the tools to do the latter.

Here's what you need to understand: Thinking quickly and strategically isn't about knowing everything. It's about knowing what to learn, how to link it, and how to leverage it for immediate results.

The 3L Method isn't just a strategy—it's a mindset. If you're serious about being a modern leader, this is where it starts. Learn faster, link deeper, and leverage everything you know to create impact. This isn't about getting it right every time—it's about getting it right faster and more effectively than your competition. Now, get out there and start practicing.

Strategy 2: Your 20 Percent Focus

Stop. Focus. Pay attention to what matters. Forget everything else.

The 20% Focus Framework isn't some theory you'll learn, forget, and never apply again. It's a brutal, no-nonsense tool that will redefine how you work and what you prioritize. Here's the deal: 20% of your actions create the majority of the value. The rest? It's typically a waste of time. If you're still bogged down in irrelevant tasks, you're not working smart—you're busy. There's a big difference.

This framework is the wake-up call your productivity needs. It's not for the faint of heart or the ones who want to "do everything well." If you're too busy trying to cover all bases, you're doing it wrong. The key to working at a high level is identifying what will move the needle—what's the critical 20% Focus that delivers the majority of results, and then hammering that out.

THE 20% FOCUS FRAMEWORK: It's Simple but Effective

The 20% Focus Framework is simple. But don't mistake simple for easy. The idea is that the majority of results come from 20% of your effort. It works everywhere—business, life, even your personal time. But here's the thing: you need to be able to identify your 20% Focus.

In my coaching experience, I've seen leaders waste time on tasks that don't move them forward. They get caught up in the weeds, dealing with non-critical stuff just to feel productive. I once worked with a senior leader in a multinational firm, whose team was spending hours on reports no one ever used. The truth? Those reports were work that was yielding 20% of the results. By cutting those out and focusing on the tasks that drove growth—client meetings, strategy development, and team innovation—they began to see a sharp increase in productivity.

Actionable Insight: Take a long, hard look at your calendar and to-do list. What are you spending your time on that doesn't matter? If it doesn't impact your bottom line, your people, or your personal development—cut it. You can always outsource, delegate, or ignore it.

IDENTIFYING THE CRITICAL 20% Focus

In the last coaching session I ran for a high-potential leader at an energy company, I had him break down his current tasks into two lists: one for things that directly impacted his KPIs, and the other for tasks that were simply time-consuming but didn't contribute significantly.

We identified a pattern: a lot of time was being spent on operations and admin work, things that were important but didn't push the business forward. When we applied the 20% Focus Framework lens, the top 20% of his tasks were the ones that directly linked to leadership—driving strategic initiatives, aligning with stakeholders, and coaching his team.

He quickly realized that the more he focused on empowering his team to take on the operational workload, the more time he had to focus on what truly mattered. Within three months, his team was more self-sufficient, and his personal output on strategic projects skyrocketed.

Actionable Insight: List your top three tasks each day, each week, and each month that will give you the highest returns. How can you maximize your focus on those three tasks? Do you need to outsource, delegate, or even drop the rest? If you don't know what the 20% Focus is, you're wasting time.

PRIORITIZE, DELEGATE, or Eliminate

This is where the rubber meets the road. You don't have unlimited time, energy, or resources. You have to make choices. Prioritizing is easy in theory, but when you're in the weeds, it's easy to get distracted.

I once ran an assessment center for a group of leaders at a major telecom company. One of the candidates, a middle manager, had too many competing priorities. He was spread thin—too many meetings, too many emails, too many projects he couldn't delegate. He was always stressed, but nothing was moving forward.

We sat down, did a deep dive into his schedule, and broke it down with the 20% Focus Framework. We identified that the high-value tasks were all strategic, yet he spent majority of his time managing the day-to-day noise. We cut out the waste—meetings that didn't require his input, tasks that could be delegated, and priorities that didn't align with the company's goals. The results? A calmer, more focused manager who was able to take charge of the big-picture decisions that actually mattered.

Actionable Insight: When you're overwhelmed, start by dumping everything onto a list. Then, ruthlessly eliminate or delegate anything that doesn't align with your top 20% Focus. Stop being the bottleneck. If you can't delegate, find a way to automate. If you can't automate, question whether it's worth doing at all.

AVOID THE SUNK COST Fallacy

Let me put it bluntly: you've probably already invested too much time in things that don't matter. You're stuck in the sunk cost fallacy—just because you've been working on something for hours, days, or even months, doesn't mean you should keep working on it.

In one of my sessions with a senior executive, we discussed a project that had consumed her entire team's attention. They were deep into it, but the results were minimal. They'd already invested so much time and energy, they couldn't bear to stop, even though it was clear it was a lost cause. The classic sunk cost fallacy.

Here's the reality: if it's not going to give you the return you expect, stop wasting your time. Cut your losses. Focus on what will work.

Actionable Insight: Don't let past investments (money, time, effort) cloud your judgment. If something's not working, drop it. Be ruthless. The faster you can cut out the waste, the faster you can focus on what actually matters.

THE POWER OF SAYING No

This isn't just a strategy; it's a mindset. Too many people, especially leaders, are terrified of saying no. They say yes to every meeting, every request, every task that comes their way. But here's the truth: you can't do it all. Saying no doesn't make you weak or indecisive. It makes you smart.

In one of my recent assessments, a senior leader was drowning in requests. Every time someone asked for his help, he said yes. He didn't want to seem unhelpful, but it was killing his ability to focus on the things that truly mattered. The solution was simple: teach him to say no.

We used the 20% Focus Framework to look at what was important, and then built a boundary strategy around saying no to anything that didn't contribute. By setting clear boundaries, he cleared his schedule, was able to focus on high-impact initiatives, and started getting results in ways he hadn't before.

Actionable Insight: Start saying no. No to meetings that don't move the needle. No to tasks that drain your time without a meaningful return. Say no until your focus is razor-sharp. Saying no is a power move, not a weakness.

EXECUTION IS EVERYTHING

The biggest pitfall in the 20% Focus Framework is that people overcomplicate it. They understand the concept but never put it into practice. They write their lists, make their priorities, but never take action.

I've seen this in action during assessments, especially when leaders get so caught up in theory that they don't make decisions or execute. They're paralyzed by the need to get everything perfect. Here's the reality: execution is everything. You can't afford to get caught in overthinking. If you want results, you need to start making decisions and take action—today.

Actionable Insight: Don't just make a list. Start executing. Get out of your head and into action. Your 20% Focus won't matter if you don't take consistent, bold steps toward the critical tasks.

CONCLUSION

The 20% Focus Framework is a game-changer—but only if you embrace it. Stop wasting time. Prioritize the 20% Focus that matters and eliminate the rest. It's simple, but it's not easy. To make it work, you'll need to be brutal, decisive, and smart. If you're stuck in the weeds, it's time to cut your losses and focus on what will actually get results.

Now go, and execute. Time is ticking.

Strategy 3: Reverse Mapping

Here's a tough truth: too many people dive into projects and tasks with no clear roadmap. They set out with enthusiasm, but without a clear vision of the end game. They waste time, lose direction, and make decisions that leave them spinning their wheels. If you want to avoid this, you need to stop starting at the beginning. Reverse Mapping is the strategy that flips the process on its head and forces you to focus on what matters—where you want to end up. And it works. Every time.

REVERSE MAPPING: WHAT It Is, Why It Works, and How It Will Save You

Reverse Mapping is exactly what it sounds like: you start with the end goal in mind, then work your way backward to identify the steps required to get there. It's simple but powerful. Instead of blindly moving forward hoping that you'll eventually get to the right destination, you take control by clearly understanding where you're going and then plotting a direct path backward.

Why does this work? Simple: when you can see the end goal, you can anticipate potential roadblocks, identify critical steps, and avoid unnecessary detours. In business, leadership, or any high-stakes decision-making process, knowing where you're going allows you to act with laser-focused intention. The clearer you are about the end state, the clearer your path forward becomes. If you don't have that clarity? You're just wasting time.

THINK FAST. THINK SMART. THINK BOLD. THINK BEYOND.

LET'S BREAK IT DOWN with a Real-World Example

I've worked with a lot of people who get stuck in the details—especially in complex leadership decisions. Let me tell you about one situation with a senior executive in a big company. This individual was under pressure to restructure a division and had no idea where to start. His team was fragmented, morale was low, and there was confusion all around.

When we started talking, he was focused on all the small, tactical problems. He was bogged down in the specifics of team assignments, restructuring the workflows, and worrying about who might leave. The problem? He hadn't clearly defined the end goal for the team. He wasn't sure what the "success" of this reorganization would even look like.

So, I flipped it on him and asked, "What does success look like when this is all over? What does the team need to accomplish by the end of the year?"

The conversation shifted from focusing on immediate actions to defining the big picture. He started thinking about what he wanted the division to look like three months down the road—what specific outcomes he wanted, what metrics mattered, and how the team should be performing.

Once we had that vision, the rest was easy. He could now map backwards: "What do I need to do to make that vision real? What are the key milestones? What's the timeline for each action? What resources will I need?" It became clear quickly that the real problem wasn't the structure—it was the lack of alignment, motivation, and clarity.

By mapping backwards from the end goal, we identified exactly what needed to happen first, second, and third. More importantly, we avoided getting distracted by peripheral issues. He had his path, and his focus was razor-sharp.

HOW TO USE REVERSE Mapping

Step 1: Visualize the End Goal

The first thing you need to do is take a step back. Picture the final outcome you want to achieve. Where are you headed? Whether it's a business objective, a project, or a leadership goal, start with the finish line in mind. What does success look like when you get there? Write it down.

Example: Let's say you're leading a team through a major project, and the end goal is to launch a new product by the end of Q3. Your end goal is clear: a successful product launch. But now ask yourself: What does "success" look like? How do you define it? This isn't just about launching a product; it's about hitting specific sales targets, getting a certain market share, or receiving feedback from customers.

Step 2: Work Backwards to Identify Milestones

Once you've defined the end goal, work your way back. Identify the key milestones or actions that must happen before you reach the goal. These steps should be logical, and there should be no ambiguity about their importance.

Example: For the product launch, the milestones might include developing the product prototype, conducting market research, testing the product with a focus group, finalizing packaging, and securing retail partnerships. Each of these milestones should have a clear deadline.

Step 3: Identify Potential Barriers and Challenges

Now that you know the milestones, take a moment to think about potential roadblocks. What could prevent you from hitting those milestones? Could there be resource shortages, team challenges, or unforeseen market shifts? Spot these obstacles early, so you're not blindsided when they arise.

Example: A potential barrier to your product launch might be the unexpected delay in manufacturing. If you identify this risk early, you can develop a contingency plan. Maybe you plan to accelerate earlier stages of the product development or keep a close eye on manufacturing timelines to ensure the schedule stays on track.

Step 4: Plan Your Actions

Now that you've identified the key steps and potential obstacles, you can start planning your actions. You should be able to answer the following questions for each milestone: What needs to happen to make this milestone a reality? What resources or people are required? What's the timeline?

Example: For the product prototype, you may need to pull together a team of engineers, designers, and product testers. You might also need a specific budget allocated to R&D. The plan should be actionable, and every decision should be aligned with hitting the next milestone.

Step 5: Execute with Intention

Once your map is laid out, execute the plan with purpose. Work backward to progress forward. The biggest mistake people make at this stage is skipping steps, assuming they'll "catch up" later. It doesn't work like that. Stay disciplined. Work the plan, stay focused on the milestones, and adjust as necessary.

Example: When I was coaching a senior leader managing a company-wide transformation, we used Reverse Mapping to identify and address early gaps. The initial gap was clear communication across departments. By mapping backwards, we could quickly identify the need for a communications team and set up processes to ensure every team leader had up-to-date information.

Step 6: Measure and Adjust

Reverse Mapping isn't a one-and-done strategy. It's iterative. Once you hit each milestone, assess whether you're still on track. If you encounter new obstacles, adapt your plan and move forward.

Example: Back to the product launch—if market research reveals that your original assumptions about customer preferences were wrong, don't panic. Adjust the product design, marketing plan, or sales targets accordingly. Keep moving forward with the new, adjusted roadmap.

WHY IT WORKS

Reverse Mapping works because it forces you to think strategically. It keeps you focused on the outcome, not the distractions. Too many leaders and organizations waste energy on random tasks that don't get them closer to the finish line. Reverse Mapping stops that by keeping you focused on what matters—where you want to go.

In my experience, those who use this strategy consistently tend to hit their goals more efficiently. They spend less time in meetings, fewer hours in the weeds, and more time doing the things that move the needle. It's that simple.

So, take a moment right now: what goal are you working toward? Have you Reverse Mapped your way there yet? If not, do it now. And make sure you're clear on where you're going. You'll save yourself a ton of headaches, and you'll move forward with far greater speed and precision.

Strategy 4: The 5C Questioning Model

You've heard it a thousand times—problem-solving is critical to success. But how often have you tackled a problem and ended up making it worse? How many times have you spent hours trying to solve something, only to realize you were focused on the wrong thing all along?

Enter the 5C Questioning Model. This simple framework will prevent you from spinning your wheels and wasting time. It forces you to pause, analyze, and ensure that you're solving the right problem, not just reacting to a surface-level issue. No more band-aid fixes. If you want clarity and to solve problems like a pro, this model is your new best friend.

WHAT IS THE 5C MODEL?

1. Clarify – What's the real issue?
2. Cause – Why did this happen?
3. Choices – What options do I have?
4. Consequences – What are the risks and outcomes?
5. Commitment – What decision will I act on?

Simple. Powerful. And it works. Let's talk about why this model is worth your time and how to make it part of your everyday approach.

CLARIFY – WHAT'S THE real issue?

You've probably been in that situation where you're stuck in a conversation, or worse, an entire meeting, solving the wrong problem. Here's the thing—if you don't get to the real issue, you're just wasting your time.

It's like trying to fix a car that's out of gas instead of noticing the engine is broken. The key is understanding the problem before jumping to conclusions or making decisions.

Let's say you're coaching a leader in your team who is constantly getting feedback about their communication style. The leader's instinct is to brush it off as a personality clash, but in reality, the problem may be a lack of empathy in their communication. They think they're being efficient, but they come off as blunt or even abrasive. Clarifying the real issue here isn't about arguing over whether they're right or wrong—it's about diving deep into the feedback and understanding what's truly causing friction.

Here's where the problem often lies: many people jump to conclusions and focus on symptoms, not the root cause. If you don't understand the real issue, you're not going to solve anything.

CAUSE – WHY DID THIS happen?

Once you have clarity on the issue, you've got to figure out what caused it. If you skip this step, you're back to square one. It's like going to a doctor with symptoms but not getting a diagnosis. You need to dig deeper and understand the underlying reasons behind the problem. Without that, you're just slapping a band-aid on a deeper wound.

For instance, in an assessment center for a leadership position, I once had a candidate who was struggling with team management. He was getting frustrated with his team's lack of initiative and thought it was due to their laziness. But when we peeled back the layers, it turned out the real cause was his management style. His team didn't feel empowered to make decisions. His constant micromanaging crushed their confidence.

It's easy to point fingers. "They're not performing." "They're not listening." But before you start placing blame, ask yourself: Why did this happen?

Once you've identified the root cause, you're already miles ahead. You've stopped wasting time on false assumptions and now have the right problem to solve.

CHOICES – WHAT OPTIONS do I have?

Now comes the fun part: options. So many people jump to solutions right away, thinking they've cracked the code. Big mistake. If you want to find the best solution, you need to step back and explore multiple options. Don't be lazy. Don't rush.

For example, imagine you're helping a client who's in a leadership position but is facing resistance to a new strategic direction. It's not about picking the first solution you think of. Do you immediately tell them to "fix their communication"? Maybe. But first, what other options exist? Should they hold a team workshop to better explain the vision? Should they individually meet with key stakeholders to get buy-in? Or should they tweak the strategy to address concerns that have been raised?

You need to evaluate all possible choices, not just the one that seems easiest or most obvious. This is your time to think creatively. There's no room for laziness here. If you don't explore your choices, you'll end up going with the first option—and that may not be the best one.

In my experience, many leaders, especially at the senior level, struggle with this part of the process. They tend to make snap decisions because they're pressured for time or feel they need to act quickly. But the truth is, they often end up making poor decisions that could have been avoided if they'd just given themselves a bit more time to explore alternatives.

CONSEQUENCES – WHAT are the risks and outcomes?

Okay, you've got your options. Now it's time to ask yourself: What are the consequences? What's the worst that could happen if you choose each option?

One client of mine, a mid-level manager, was facing a conflict between two of his team members. They'd been arguing over responsibilities, and it was starting to affect the overall morale. He had two options: Step in and mediate or let them sort it out themselves.

On the surface, the first option seemed like the logical choice. He could step in and resolve it quickly. But what would happen if he did? He might alienate one of the team members, further escalating the conflict. Or he could give them space, which might lead to more arguments, but it could also build their problem-solving skills. He had to weigh the consequences of each action.

In my coaching sessions, I often ask clients to list out the consequences of each option. Not just the immediate effects, but the long-term ones too. What happens next? What does this mean down the line?

It's about being strategic, not impulsive. If you don't think through the consequences of your decisions, you're asking for trouble. And when the fallout happens, don't say I didn't warn you.

COMMITMENT – WHAT DECISION will I act on?

Now that you've done all the legwork—clarified the issue, identified the cause, explored options, and weighed the consequences—it's time to commit. Stop procrastinating. Stop overthinking. Choose a course of action and act on it.

A client I worked with recently was struggling with a leadership transition. His team was divided, some were embracing change, others were resisting it. He knew he had to make a decision on how to proceed but kept delaying it because he was worried about making the wrong choice.

After we walked through the 5C process, it was clear: He needed to communicate a clear vision for the future and take charge of the transition. It wasn't about perfecting every detail—it was about committing to a decision and executing it with confidence. The longer he delayed, the more uncertainty and resistance brewed in the team.

THINK FAST. THINK SMART. THINK BOLD. THINK BEYOND.

If you don't commit, you'll remain stuck in analysis paralysis. You'll overthink, second-guess, and eventually, you'll lose momentum. Decide. Commit. Execute.

WHY THIS WORKS

This model works because it forces you to take a structured, disciplined approach to problem-solving. It's not just about being reactive; it's about taking control of the situation and thinking through it in a methodical way.

It's easy to get swept up in the chaos of daily challenges. Everyone has problems. Everyone has urgent fires to put out. But if you want to be a problem solver—not just a problem reactor—you need a framework. You need structure.

And the 5C Questioning Model delivers exactly that. By forcing you to clarify, understand causes, explore options, evaluate consequences, and commit, you ensure that you're solving the right problem and making the best possible decision. No more knee-jerk reactions. No more sloppy decision-making. Just clear, effective action.

Now, get to work.

Strategy 5: The Pivot Perspective Technique

You're stuck. Something's not moving. No matter how much you push or plan, you just can't get ahead. This is the moment where most people buckle down, grind harder, or double down on the same approach. But the truth is, that's a dumb move. When you're stuck, the best thing you can do isn't to try harder; it's to shift. That's where the Pivot Perspective Technique comes in.

When you hit a roadblock, shift your perspective. It's time to stop thinking about the problem in the same tired way and look at it from a new angle. This is how you unlock fresh ideas. Don't just look within your own industry or mindset. Ask yourself, "How would someone from a completely different field solve this problem?"

The Pivot Perspective Technique forces you to change your thinking, and in doing so, it unlocks possibilities you would have never considered if you stayed in the same lane. It's like putting on a new pair of glasses, seeing the world from a different view, and suddenly, everything makes sense.

HERE'S HOW IT WORKS:

1. Identify the problem. First, be crystal clear about what you're up against. What's the issue? Is it a problem with communication? A financial crunch? A resource bottleneck? Define the problem in sharp terms.

2. Switch perspectives. This is the pivot. Now, ask how someone from an unrelated field—say, a marketer, a finance professional, or an en-

gineer—would solve the problem. How might they approach it? What strategies would they use? It's about breaking free from your own limitations and looking at things with fresh eyes.

3. Brainstorm. Once you've shifted perspectives, go wild with ideas. Let the brainstorm flow, uninhibited by the usual "this is how we've always done it" mindset. Get creative. The goal here isn't to solve the problem in one sitting but to come up with as many fresh perspectives as you can. The more diverse your solutions, the better.

4. Focus on practical actions. The final step in the pivot is about returning to reality. Now that you've come up with fresh, creative ideas, you need to refocus and figure out what will actually work. Which of those ideas are actionable and realistic? Get down to brass tacks and start making a move.

WHY IT WORKS:

Because conventional thinking is, well, conventional. It's too easy to fall into old habits and repetitive solutions. By forcing yourself to shift perspectives and rethink problems, you disrupt the routine and uncover innovative solutions. The Pivot Perspective Technique is like rebooting your brain, and when you do that, you're bound to see things in a whole new light.

In my coaching experience, I've seen this technique turn whole teams around. Let's take a look at one example.

EXAMPLE FROM COACHING:

I was coaching a leadership team from a regional manufacturing firm. They were facing a serious productivity issue. The lines were running slower than expected, and they couldn't figure out why. They tried everything—firing up morale boosters, pushing employees harder, tweaking schedules—but nothing was working.

When I introduced the Pivot Perspective Technique, I had them start by stepping outside the manufacturing mindset. Instead of focusing on fixing the assembly line, I asked them to think like a marketer. I told them, "How would a marketer improve a product launch when the first attempt is failing?"

This might sound like a stretch, but hear me out. Marketers don't just try harder—they analyze the market, understand the consumer's needs, adjust messaging, and tweak the product to appeal better. So why not do the same here? Instead of pushing harder, why not analyze the whole process from a new angle?

The team started brainstorming with a new perspective. They moved away from pushing employees harder and instead looked at the entire process from a customer satisfaction viewpoint. They wondered: what did the customers (the end users of the product) really care about? How could they improve the product's overall appeal by streamlining the process?

The result? They identified inefficiencies in how product features were being communicated on the line, and they restructured how they packaged and delivered the product to their customers. Instead of adding more strain on workers, they focused on making the product delivery clearer and more efficient. The result was an increase in overall productivity in just several weeks.

That's the power of a pivot.

REAL-WORLD EXAMPLE:

Let's talk about another example—this time from an assessment center I ran. I had a candidate, let's call him Tom, who was struggling with an issue in his current role. Tom was working in a fast-paced logistics environment where his team was handling multiple projects simultaneously. The problem? He had hit a wall in terms of team performance. No matter what he tried, his team's output wasn't improving.

When we did a role-play exercise, I had him apply the Pivot Perspective Technique. Instead of trying to "fix" the team by exerting more pressure, I had him take a step back and think about how a financial analyst would approach the issue. Financial analysts are constantly working with data, evaluating trends, and identifying areas to reduce waste. So, I asked Tom, "What if you looked at your team's output the way a financial analyst would? What data can you pull to identify the real gaps?"

Tom spent a few minutes thinking about it. He realized that by focusing on metrics like time to complete tasks and communication breakdowns, he could pinpoint where the delays were happening. Armed with this new data-driven mindset, he restructured his team's workflow. The results? He began to see an improvement in efficiency over the next few months.

THE KEY TO MASTERING the Pivot Perspective:

The hardest part of the Pivot Perspective Technique is forcing yourself to stop and shift. It feels uncomfortable because it goes against the grain of traditional problem-solving. But that's the whole point: it breaks the mold. The best solutions come when you take a step back, challenge your assumptions, and think about things from a different angle.

In my experience, leaders who are stuck in their ways—the ones who think their way is the only way—will never get ahead. They're too entrenched in their own biases and methods. But those who embrace the Pivot Perspective Technique can constantly evolve, adapt, and stay ahead of the game.

HOW TO APPLY THE PIVOT Perspective Technique:

1. Start with a problem. Pinpoint the issue clearly and without overcomplicating it.

2. Switch perspectives. Consider how someone from a completely different field or role would solve the problem.

3. Brainstorm wildly. Come up with a range of solutions without worrying about whether they're "realistic" yet.

4. Refocus on practicality. Narrow down your ideas to what's actionable and effective.

5. Take action. Implement the best solution immediately. Don't wait for "perfect" conditions. Make it happen.

THIS TECHNIQUE ISN'T just a creative exercise; it's a tactical weapon. It's about looking at problems differently, finding solutions where others see none, and being flexible enough to adapt when the old ways don't work. So, stop banging your head against the wall. Pivot, think differently, and make it happen.

Strategy 6: Scenario Sprints

Here's the deal: if you want to move fast, you need to get comfortable with making decisions in the face of uncertainty. You can't wait around for the perfect conditions to arrive; that's a surefire way to miss the boat. One of the most effective tools for making quick decisions in unpredictable situations is Scenario Sprints.

This method is about forcing yourself into rapid decision-making. You'll quickly generate three potential scenarios—Best Case, Worst Case, and Most Likely Case—then work through how you would respond to each. It's all about being prepared for multiple outcomes, so when the unexpected happens, you're already one step ahead. You're not just planning for one path; you're ready for all of them.

HERE'S HOW TO MAKE this work for you:

1. Generate 3 Scenarios. Don't get fancy. You don't need to predict every single outcome. Just focus on these three:

   o Best Case: What's the optimal outcome? Picture everything going right. What's the ideal result if everything falls into place?

   o Worst Case: What's the worst thing that could happen? If everything falls apart, what does that look like? What's the disaster scenario you want to avoid?

   o Most Likely Case: What's realistic? This is where most of your focus should go. Based on current information, what's the most probable outcome?

2. Prepare Responses for Each Scenario. Don't just sit around and hope for the best. You need a plan for each of the three scenarios. In fact, you should have a response ready for all three in 15 minutes or less. Here's the trick: move fast. Don't get bogged down with overthinking. Just identify key actions for each scenario and write them down.

3. Execute with Confidence. You've got your scenarios. Now it's time to act. Don't second-guess yourself. Whatever happens, you're ready to handle it. If things go better than expected, fantastic. If things go sideways, you've already got a backup plan. The most important thing is to move fast and make a decision.

WHY IT WORKS:

Scenario Sprints give you a structured way to make decisions quickly. We all know that nothing is ever certain, so you can't afford to freeze up when things don't go as planned. When you visualize multiple potential outcomes, you prepare yourself mentally for anything that could come your way. This removes the fear of the unknown because you've already mapped out a path for each possibility. You're no longer reacting; you're acting.

In my coaching experience, I've seen this strategy separate the leaders who thrive under pressure from those who crumble. When you have a plan for the worst case, you'll be far less paralyzed by fear. And when things go better than expected, you'll be able to seize those opportunities because you've already prepped for success.

EXAMPLE FROM COACHING:

I had a client—let's call him Mike—who was overseeing a major restructuring in his company. The organization was cutting costs, and the process was creating chaos. Mike was under pressure from all sides, with employees anxious about layoffs and upper management demanding immediate results.

Mike initially tried to approach the situation with a singular focus on the "best case" scenario—everything would go smoothly, and employees would be happy with the transition. But guess what? The best-case scenario didn't happen. There were hiccups. The new structure was met with resistance, and employees were skeptical.

That's when I introduced him to Scenario Sprints. Instead of obsessing over a single outcome, I had Mike prepare for three scenarios:

1. Best Case: The restructure goes smoothly. Employees adapt quickly, and the new system increases productivity. Mike has a positive feedback meeting with the leadership team to highlight the success.

2. Worst Case: The restructure fails. There's resistance, productivity drops, and people start leaving. Mike needs to move quickly to fix morale, stabilize the team, and reduce turnover.

3. Most Likely Case: There will be some initial resistance, but the restructure will eventually gain traction. Productivity will take a slight dip, but the team will start adapting over time. Mike's challenge will be managing this transition period and ensuring that communication remains clear.

Once Mike had these scenarios, we worked together to draft responses for each. If the worst case happened, he was ready to meet with the team, address concerns, and offer support. If the best case happened, he had an action plan to celebrate success and leverage momentum. And for the most likely case, Mike focused on ensuring clear communication throughout the process and providing consistent updates to keep the team on track.

Within just a few days, things started improving. Mike was more confident because he wasn't just guessing what would happen next—he had a plan for every possibility. He wasn't reacting to the situation; he was proactively managing it.

REAL-WORLD EXAMPLE:

Another case came from a training program I ran for a group of leaders from a large retail organization. Their company was launching a new product line, and the team was tasked with planning the rollout. The group was high-performing, but they were overly optimistic. They believed the product would fly off the shelves, and there was little planning for potential pitfalls.

I brought the Scenario Sprint technique into the room to get the group to think critically. I told them: "Stop assuming the best. Prepare for the worst."

They quickly generated three scenarios:

1. Best Case: The product launch exceeds expectations. Customers love it, and sales soar. The team can build on this success and expand the product line further.

2. Worst Case: The product launch flops. Customers are unimpressed, and sales are slow. The team has to move quickly to salvage the launch, maybe even pull the product and relaunch it after tweaking the offering.

3. Most Likely Case: The product launch meets expectations. Sales are decent, but the company has to work hard to maintain interest over time. The team needs to stay proactive and manage marketing efforts post-launch to keep the buzz alive.

In less than 20 minutes, the team had a clear plan for each scenario. They adjusted their marketing strategies, lined up backup plans for handling poor sales, and even started preparing for what the product might need if customer feedback was negative. When the product launched, it didn't hit the heights they hoped for, but they were prepared. They implemented the "worst case" plan, tweaked the product based on feedback, and relaunched successfully.

The Scenario Sprint saved them from complete failure. Without this structured thinking, the team could have floundered, reacting haphazardly to each challenge. Instead, they executed with precision.

THINK FAST. THINK SMART. THINK BOLD. THINK BEYOND.

HOW TO APPLY SCENARIO Sprints:

1. Identify the problem or decision. Whatever you're facing, be clear about what you need to solve or decide.

2. Generate three possible scenarios. Think of the best-case, worst-case, and most-likely outcomes. Be realistic and creative.

3. Plan responses. Don't just hope for the best. Write out concrete actions for each scenario. What will you do if the worst happens? How will you handle the best? And what steps will you take when things go as expected?

4. Act. Execute the plan. No hesitation. You've got responses for every possible outcome, so stop wasting time and make it happen.

5. Review. After you execute, review the situation. Did the worst-case scenario happen? Did the best-case scenario come through? Use what you've learned to adjust for the future.

IN THE END, THE POINT of Scenario Sprints isn't to predict the future—it's to make sure you're ready for whatever comes. You're not guessing. You're preparing. Fast. It's all about reducing uncertainty and getting ahead of problems before they snowball. When you get comfortable planning for all outcomes, you're going to make better, faster decisions. And that's what leadership is all about. Don't get caught flat-footed. Plan for the best, brace for the worst, and execute the hell out of it.

Strategy 7: THINK Grid

Here's the problem with most decision-making: people don't think it through. They rush to conclusions, make decisions based on emotions, and skip over critical aspects of what's at stake. They don't see the bigger picture. And then they wonder why things fall apart later. Well, guess what? The THINK Grid is here to fix that mess. It's time to stop reacting on impulse and start making decisions with structure, clarity, and purpose.

The THINK Grid isn't some fluffy, feel-good concept. It's a simple, no-nonsense tool that helps you evaluate decisions from all the important angles. This strategy isn't about making decisions faster—it's about making better ones. It's about clarity. It's about taking a step back, looking at the full picture, and making sure you've covered all your bases before jumping in.

WHY IT WORKS

The THINK Grid works because it forces you to slow down and assess every decision from five critical perspectives. When you're about to make a call, it's easy to get bogged down in the heat of the moment. Emotions take over. You start worrying about what's in front of you, not the bigger implications. The THINK Grid cuts through the noise by forcing you to look at things in a comprehensive, logical way.

LET'S BREAK IT DOWN:

THINK FAST. THINK SMART. THINK BOLD. THINK BEYOND.

1. Tactical – What's the short-term plan? What needs to happen right now to move things forward?

2. Holistic – How does this fit into the bigger picture? What are the long-term consequences of this decision?

3. Immediate – What needs to be done immediately? What's urgent, and what can wait?

4. Next – What's the next logical step after this one? What's the follow-up action to ensure success?

5. Key – What's the critical success factor in this situation? What needs to happen for everything else to fall into place?

By answering these five questions before making a decision, you're ensuring that your actions aren't knee-jerk reactions. You're bringing logic, structure, and foresight into play. And when you use this grid consistently, you start making better decisions—ones that align with your goals, your values, and your big-picture strategy.

APPLYING THE THINK Grid in Real Life

Let me give you an example of how this works in real life. I coached a leader in a large corporation who was facing a major staffing issue. One of their key team members was underperforming, and the leader was about to pull the trigger and let them go. Emotionally, the leader was ready to act—they were frustrated, the person wasn't meeting expectations, and the team was getting restless. But instead of rushing into the decision, we applied the THINK Grid.

Here's how the leader thought through the decision:

- Tactical: What needs to happen right now? The leader recognized they needed to have a serious conversation with the employee to understand the root cause of the performance issues.

- Holistic: How does this fit into the bigger picture? They realized that firing this employee would disrupt the team's dynamic and possibly cause a loss of morale. It would also create a leadership gap that would take time to fill.

• Immediate: What's the next step? The leader decided the immediate action was to initiate a performance review and coach the employee on how to improve.

• Next: What's the next step after that? If the employee didn't improve after a set period, the next step would be to reassess the situation and explore whether a different role would be a better fit for them.

• Key: What's the critical success factor? The key was to preserve the team's morale and minimize disruption, while still holding the underperforming employee accountable for their actions.

By taking a step back and applying the THINK Grid, this leader made a more informed decision. They didn't rush into firing someone; instead, they implemented a clear action plan that took into account both the short-term and long-term implications of their decision. In the end, the employee improved, and the team's performance didn't skip a beat.

THINKING IN LAYERS

One of the big advantages of the THINK Grid is that it forces you to think in layers. Most people think in a straight line: what's the problem? What's the solution? That's it. They don't account for the nuances, the short-term fixes versus the long-term benefits, or the ripple effects of their choices.

The THINK Grid makes you slow down and think through each layer of the decision-making process. It's not just about acting—it's about taking a comprehensive approach. For example, let's say you're trying to launch a new product. It sounds like a good idea, right? But here's the reality: if you only think about the tactical side of things (i.e., launching the product), you're missing a massive chunk of the puzzle.

IF YOU USE THE THINK Grid, you might realize:

- Tactical: Yes, launching the product is important, but what immediate steps need to happen to ensure you have the right distribution channels, marketing materials, and pricing models in place?
- Holistic: How does this launch align with your brand values, your overall business strategy, and your long-term vision? Will it build the reputation you want?
- Immediate: Is the product ready for launch, or are there last-minute tweaks that need to happen?
- Next: What's the next stage after launch? How will you handle customer feedback, adjust your marketing efforts, and respond to market demands?
- Key: What's the critical success factor? Is it the timing of the launch, the customer experience, or your ability to scale production?

Once you apply the THINK Grid, the decision-making process becomes more structured and strategic. You're thinking not just about getting the product out the door, but also about how it fits into your bigger objectives and how it will impact everything from customer perception to brand longevity.

AVOIDING COMMON PITFALLS

So here's the deal: most people don't use the THINK Grid because they don't want to slow down and think. They're busy. They want to act fast, make a decision, and move on. But here's the thing: rushing decisions doesn't mean faster results. It means poor outcomes. And the consequences of poor decisions ripple out and affect everything down the line.

I've seen it in coaching sessions countless times—leaders rushing decisions, skipping over critical thinking steps, and ending up with a mess.

It could be anything from hiring the wrong person to making a business move that disrupts the entire company's vision. But when leaders take a moment to slow down, apply the THINK Grid, and evaluate decisions from multiple perspectives, the results are night and day.

One of the leaders I worked with had this tendency to make snap decisions when it came to hiring. They were moving fast, getting people in seats, but not thinking through how these new hires would fit into the overall company culture. The result? High turnover, dissatisfaction, and a lot of wasted resources. When we started using the THINK Grid in the hiring process, they took a step back. They considered the tactical (job requirements), the holistic (company culture), the immediate (pressing needs), the next steps (training and onboarding), and the key factor (long-term employee retention). This approach transformed their hiring process and, ultimately, their company's employee satisfaction.

CONCLUSION: THINK, Don't Blink

The THINK Grid isn't some fancy model for academic types—it's for leaders, managers, and anyone who's serious about making better decisions. It's about slowing down long enough to think through every angle before acting.

If you're someone who just jumps into decisions without thinking about the bigger picture or the potential outcomes, you're setting yourself up for failure. If you're someone who's tired of making decisions that feel rushed, only to realize you missed a critical point later, then the THINK Grid is your solution.

Stop making decisions on autopilot. Apply the THINK Grid, and start making decisions that are smarter, more strategic, and more aligned with your goals. Don't just act—act with intention. The results will speak for themselves.

Strategy 8: The Connecting Connectivity

If there's one truth about the world we live in, it's this—nothing exists in isolation. Everything connects. Every decision, every action, and every outcome is part of a larger web of cause and effect. Yet most people fail to see the connections. They look at events, problems, and opportunities like they're dots scattered across a page—random and unrelated. But the best thinkers? They don't just see the dots. They connect them. They see patterns, relationships, and invisible threads tying everything together.

This is what Connecting Connectivity is all about. It's about training yourself to think beyond the obvious and dive deeper into the relationships between ideas, events, and outcomes. It's about asking, "What led to this?" and "What might this trigger next?" instead of just reacting to what's in front of you. In a world where complexity is the norm, this ability isn't just useful—it's essential.

Let's be clear. Connecting Connectivity isn't about overanalyzing or chasing conspiracy theories. It's about sharpening your ability to recognize patterns, predict ripple effects, and anticipate outcomes before they happen. It's about refusing to make decisions in isolation and training yourself to think in layers—cause, effect, ripple, consequence.

You're not just solving problems. You're untangling them.

THE LAYERS OF CONNECTIVITY

Imagine peeling an onion. On the surface, you see one layer. But peel it back, and there's another layer, and another. That's how connectivity works. Every event, decision, or behavior has layers. Most people stop at the surface. They see symptoms and treat them without ever looking for the root. You're going deeper. You're looking past the symptoms to uncover the cause—and then tracing the effects outward to see the bigger picture.

I once coached a senior leader who was struggling with low engagement in her team. She thought the issue was workload—too much pressure, too little time. But as we dug deeper, we saw the real problem. It wasn't the workload; it was a lack of clarity about priorities. Team members were busy, but they weren't focused on what mattered most. That confusion led to frustration, disengagement, and burnout. The workload was just a symptom. The root cause was poor communication about goals and expectations.

And the ripple effect? It extended beyond her team. Low morale started to impact collaboration across departments, slowing down progress on key projects. Once she fixed the root issue—by clarifying goals and improving communication—the engagement problem disappeared. Productivity shot up, and the ripple effect turned positive.

Lesson learned? Symptoms are never the whole story. The real issue is always buried beneath the surface. And the effects always extend further than you think.

THE RIPPLE-EFFECT RADAR

To master Connecting Connectivity, you need to train your Ripple-Effect Radar—a mental habit of asking, "What's next?" every time you make a decision or encounter a situation. Think of it as forecasting the waves caused by a stone dropped into water.

- Step 1: Identify the Immediate Impact – What's the first consequence of this decision, action, or event?
- Step 2: Predict the Secondary Ripples – What chain reactions could follow? What unintended side effects could emerge?

- Step 3: Map the Long-Term Effects – How might this decision influence the bigger picture weeks, months, or even years from now?

This isn't guesswork. It's pattern recognition. The more you practice it, the sharper your radar becomes.

One of my clients faced a hiring decision that seemed simple—bring in a new leader to fix performance issues in a struggling division. But we stepped back and ran the situation through the Ripple-Effect Radar.

Immediate impact? The division would get strong leadership and better direction.

Secondary ripples? The sudden change could unsettle existing team dynamics, leading to short-term resistance.

Long-term effects? If the new leader succeeded, the division would thrive, but failure could trigger higher turnover and set the team back even further.

By mapping out these ripples, the client realized they needed to prepare the existing team before the hire, establish a transition plan, and actively support the new leader to ensure long-term success. What looked like a straightforward fix suddenly became a strategic decision with layers of preparation.

FROM SYMPTOMS TO SYSTEMS

Connectivity isn't just about fixing problems. It's also about spotting opportunities. When you train yourself to see connections, you start recognizing how seemingly unrelated events can combine to create breakthroughs.

One of the best examples came from a leadership facilitation session I ran for mid-level managers. A leader identified a hidden connection between two seemingly unrelated processes—employee training and customer satisfaction. He realized that inconsistent onboarding was leading to mistakes on the front line, frustrating customers, and increasing complaints. No one else had made the connection because they were treating training and customer satisfaction as separate issues.

His insight led to a revamped training program that reduced errors, improved service quality, and boosted satisfaction scores. All because he didn't see problems in isolation.

THE COST OF DISCONNECTION

When you don't practice connectivity thinking, the cost is steep:

- Missed Root Causes: You waste time and resources fixing symptoms while the real problems remain hidden.
- Blind Spots: You fail to anticipate ripple effects and get blindsided by consequences you didn't see coming.
- Lost Opportunities: You miss chances to create value because you can't spot the links between people, processes, and ideas.

I've seen talented leaders fail—not because they lacked intelligence, but because they didn't train themselves to see connections. They reacted instead of anticipating. They treated problems as isolated events instead of patterns. And they paid the price in lost time, stalled growth, and missed opportunities.

FINAL THOUGHT: THINK in Webs, Not Dots

In today's world, leaders can't afford to think in straight lines. You need to think in webs—complex, layered, and deeply connected. Whether you're solving problems, leading teams, or seizing opportunities, the ability to see connections gives you an edge.

The Connecting Connectivity strategy isn't just another tool. It's a mindset—a way of approaching every challenge with the awareness that nothing exists in isolation. The leaders who thrive are the ones who train themselves to see the patterns no one else sees.

THINK FAST. THINK SMART. THINK BOLD. THINK BEYOND.

So start training. Build the muscle. Connect the dots. And then watch as your thinking, your decisions, and your results move to a whole new level.

Conclusion: Developing the Discipline to Think Fast, Think Smart, Think Bold, Think Beyond

We've covered a lot of ground in this book. You've learned strategies that can take your thinking and decision-making to the next level. But here's the hard truth: the information, the frameworks, the strategies—all of it is useless unless you have the discipline to put it into practice. This isn't about reading the book and feeling inspired for a few days. This is about committing to a mindset shift and building the habits that will help you consistently think fast, think smart, think bold, and think beyond.

And just like any skill, it's going to take work. It's going to take effort. It's going to take discipline. You can't expect to go from zero to hero without putting in the sweat and repetition. You're not going to wake up tomorrow and suddenly be able to think faster, smarter, bolder, and beyond—at least, not at the level you need to thrive in today's world. But you can absolutely get there if you put in the work. Just like exercising a muscle, you need to build the strength to think differently, act decisively, and lead with vision.

THE DISCIPLINE TO THINK Fast

Let's start with thinking fast. We've talked about how thinking fast isn't about rushing into decisions without the right preparation. It's about being ready when the time comes. It's about having the ability to

THINK FAST. THINK SMART. THINK BOLD. THINK BEYOND.

act quickly because you've already trained your brain to handle complex, high-pressure situations with clarity. This takes practice. A lot of it.

In my coaching experience, one of the most common issues I see with executives is that they freeze under pressure. When the heat is on, they hesitate, overthink, or second-guess themselves. It's natural. Our brains are wired to avoid risk and uncertainty. But the problem is, if you want to succeed in today's fast-paced world, hesitation will be your downfall. You need to be prepared to make decisions on the spot, even when the facts aren't all in. The key is to build the mental muscle that allows you to make fast, confident decisions based on your experience, intuition, and the frameworks you've developed.

It's like training for a race. At first, your sprinting technique might be clumsy. But with practice, it becomes instinctual. You don't think about the mechanics of running—you just go. It's the same with thinking fast. The more you practice making quick decisions, the more second-nature it becomes. You have to expose yourself to situations where you have to make decisions on the fly. It could be a small decision, like deciding which action to take in a meeting, or a big one, like navigating a crisis. But every decision, no matter how big or small, is an opportunity to sharpen your speed.

THE DISCIPLINE TO THINK Smart

Thinking smart is where your intellect, your experience, and your instincts come together. You have to take what you know, apply it to the situation at hand, and use your judgment to make the best call. But thinking smart isn't just about being clever or knowledgeable; it's about being resourceful and strategic.

When you think smart, you're able to sift through the noise and zero in on what matters. You recognize patterns, anticipate challenges, and take action that makes a meaningful difference. But here's the catch: this ability doesn't come automatically. It takes consistent effort to develop and refine your thinking. You have to actively seek out knowledge, ask the right questions, and surround yourself with people who challenge your thinking. You also have to practice applying that knowledge in the real world.

During one of my assessment centers, I worked with a senior leader who was an expert in finance. On paper, he was brilliant. But when it came to making decisions beyond his area of expertise—decisions that required strategic thinking or market foresight—he struggled. His intelligence wasn't enough to push him past the limits of his own expertise. We worked together to expand his thinking beyond the numbers, to see the bigger picture. We used case studies, simulations, and real-world scenarios to help him stretch his mind, to practice using his intellect in areas outside his comfort zone.

The key takeaway? Thinking smart requires intentional practice. You don't just become a smart thinker by hoping it'll happen. You need to apply your knowledge across different contexts, deliberately refining how you use what you know. You have to be curious, skeptical, and always looking for ways to improve your thinking. Over time, thinking smart becomes more intuitive. You start recognizing patterns, identifying opportunities, and making connections that others miss. But that comes with repetition. It's about making every decision a learning experience.

THE DISCIPLINE TO THINK Bold

Here's where most people fail. Thinking bold is about taking risks, challenging the status quo, and having the courage to act when others are waiting for a "safer" solution. Boldness isn't just for entrepreneurs or disruptors. It's for anyone who wants to make an impact. Whether you're leading a team, running a department, or sitting in the C-suite, thinking bold is about pushing the boundaries of what's possible.

I've worked with countless leaders who play it safe. They wait for the perfect data, the perfect conditions, or the perfect team to make a bold move. But guess what? That perfect moment never comes. Bold decisions are messy, imperfect, and uncomfortable. But they're also the decisions that change the game.

The discipline of thinking bold comes with accepting that failure is a part of the process. You're going to get things wrong. You're going to face setbacks. But that's the price you pay for progress. The key to developing the discipline to think bold is to embrace discomfort. It's about learning to move forward, even when the way isn't clear. It's about taking calculated risks, making big moves, and betting on yourself when everyone else is playing it safe.

I remember working with a client who was hesitant to make a huge strategic initiative in his business. He was afraid of the backlash, the uncertainty, and the risk involved. We had long discussions about the cost of inaction—how staying the course might lead to gradual decline, while bold moves could open up new opportunities. Ultimately, he took the risk, and the company saw a significant transformation, capturing new market share and gaining a competitive edge. It wasn't easy, but it was worth it.

The truth is, boldness takes discipline. It's about pushing through fear and doubt, and making decisions that others are too afraid to make. It's about doing what others won't and being willing to deal with the consequences. If you're not willing to be bold, you'll never truly make an impact.

THE DISCIPLINE TO THINK Beyond

Thinking beyond is where the real magic happens. This is where you get to see the world in ways that others can't. It's about looking past today's problems and thinking about tomorrow's possibilities. Thinking beyond requires vision. It requires a deep understanding of trends, opportunities, and risks, and the ability to make decisions that set you up for long-term success.

This is the most difficult of all the disciplines. It's easy to get caught up in the immediate demands of your job, the pressure of your team, or the distractions of daily life. But to think beyond, you have to rise above the noise. You have to make the conscious decision to focus on what's next, not just what's now.

I've met leaders who had the vision to see where their industry was heading long before their competitors. These leaders didn't just make decisions for today; they made decisions for tomorrow. And when tomorrow came, they were ready. The businesses that thrived were the ones that had leaders thinking beyond what was directly in front of them. They made moves that set them up for success years down the road.

The discipline to think beyond is about expanding your focus. It's about seeing the big picture and understanding how your decisions today will ripple out into the future. And that takes practice. It's about consistently asking yourself, "How will this decision impact the next five years? What's the future I'm building?" Thinking beyond is a long-term game, and you have to be patient with the process.

CONCLUSION: COMMIT to the Discipline of Thinking

Developing the discipline to think fast, think smart, think bold, and think beyond isn't something that happens overnight. It's a continuous practice. Like exercising a muscle, the more you work at it, the stronger it gets. The more you push yourself, the more you'll see the results.

But let me make this crystal clear: you'll only get better at these disciplines if you put in the work. If you're not ready to commit to the long haul, to the constant learning, to the discomfort, then don't waste your time. But if you are—if you're ready to sharpen your mind, take risks, and see the world differently—then these strategies are your blueprint for success.

Now it's up to you. Make the decision to practice these disciplines every single day. Make the decision to become the kind of thinker who

THINK FAST. THINK SMART. THINK BOLD. THINK BEYOND.

can thrive in any situation. The world won't wait for you to catch up. So get started now.

About the Author

Marako Marcus is a management consultant, coach, and public speaker with over 25 years of experience, and a reputation for being straight to the point. He helps executives, teams, and individuals face their challenges head-on, cutting through the corporate nonsense and delivering results that matter. With years of experience working with organizations of all sizes, Marako has knowledge of what's wrong with most workplaces and ideas on how to fix them—without the usual corporate jargon.

A master of tough love and tough conversations, he's a coach who asks those powerful questions, tells it like it is and makes sure you know exactly where you stand. His approach is simple: if you're not getting it done, stop whining and start acting. He's worked with leaders who need a wake-up call and teams who need someone to light a fire under them.

When he's not stirring up success in the business world, Marako unleashes his creativity as a musician and producer. Yes, he's the guy who can juggle spreadsheets and compose a killer track at the same time—proving that sharp focus can strike the right chord in both the boardroom and the studio. Marako's blend of directness and creativity makes him a unique voice in the business world—and someone you'll want to listen to.

Read more at https://linktr.ee/marakomarcusbooks.

www.ingramcontent.com/pod-product-compliance
Lightning Source LLC
Chambersburg PA
CBHW070419230526
45471CB00006B/2878